Old NEWTOWNARDS

by

John Hanna, with photographs from the Des Quail collection

An aerial view of Newtownards from around 1929, showing the centre of the town which was created when Alexander Stewart built the Market House and the Square in front of it in 1770. A cruciform street plan was made around Conway Square and the centre moved west from the Market Cross, and the parallel streets of West Street/East Street, Regent Street/Frances Street, and High Street were intersected by North Street/South Street, Mary Street and Ann Street. Later development took place mostly to the north on higher ground.

Text © John Hanna, 2004.
First published in the United Kingdom, 2004,
by Stenlake Publishing,
Telephone: 01290 551122
Printed by Cordfall Ltd, Glasgow G21 2QA

ISBN 1 84033 290 5

FURTHER READING

The books listed below were used by the author during his research. None of them are available from Stenlake Publishing. Those interested in finding out more are advised to contact their local bookshop or reference library.
Various works of the Ards Historical Society.
The Blair Mayne Association, *Glimpses of Old Newtownards*.
Trevor McCavery, *Newtown: A History of Newtownards*, White Row Press, 1994.

ACKNOWLEDGEMENTS

The author wishes to thank Elwood and Avis Miskelly of Newtownards and Noel O'Neill of the Ulster Flying Club for their assistance.

While this appears to be Helen's Tower at the Clandeboye Estate near Newtownards, closer inspection indicates French military uniforms and what is actually shown is the commemoration of the Ulster Memorial Tower in Thiepval, France, on 19 November 1921. The tower was erected in memory of the 5,500 members of the 36th Ulster Division who were killed in the Battle of the Somme. It is a replica of Helen's Tower at Clandeboye, where many of the men trained before departing to the front.

Opposite: The 'big stone' lies on the eastern shore of Strangford Lough, some 2½ miles outside Newtownards. In the past it was sometimes known as the 'Butterlump Stone'. It is 130 tons of dolerite, a glacial erratic eroded from Scrabo Hill at the time the ice cap was moving in a south-easterly direction. It has always had a religious message painted on its surface.

INTRODUCTION

The Newtownards area was first inhabited during the Stone Age, between 7000 BC and 3500 BC, and these settlers were succeeded by Neolithic farmers between 3500 BC and 2000 BC. Certainly Scrabo Hill was occupied by people of the Bronze Age prior to 300 BC, and in the Iron Age from 300 BC to AD 500. Celtic tribes then arrived from central Europe and it was to these people that St Finian brought Christianity in the sixth century AD, when he founded a monastery at Movilla to the east of present-day Newtownards.

The arrival of Viking raiders in Strangford Lough early in the ninth century, and later the O'Neills, led to the destruction of Movilla. Attacks continued with the arrival of the Normans. In February 1177 John de Courcy, an Anglo–Norman Knight, raided Ulster and after routing the Irish he was granted some lands by King Henry II. He created barons from his tenants and the area around Newtownards became part of the powerful manor of Dundonald. Henry's successor, King John, considered de Courcy to be too powerful and Hugh de Lacy was sent to dispose of him. After doing so he was granted de Courcy's land and was created Earl of Ulster in 1205. Following Norman practice, the conquered area was divided into small counties and one of these was the 'County of Blaethwyc of the Ardes'. It was within this county, around 1226, that the 'New Town of Ardes' was formed as its administrative centre.

In 1244 Walter de Burgh, Earl of Ulster, founded a monastery for Dominican friars. On its dissolution in 1541, its lands became part of Clannaboy and were owned by the O'Neills. Efforts were made by Sir Thomas Smith to establish an English settlement 'in the Great and Little Ardes', but this was opposed by the O'Neills who destroyed the town in 1572. In 1603 the English captured Con O'Neill and to secure his release he made a deal with Hugh Montgomery and another Scot, James Hamilton. Newtownards and the surrounding lands became the property of Montgomery and in 1606 he set about rebuilding the town.

Montgomery's main objectives were to inhabit the lands with English and Scots settlers, setting up weekly markets in the main population centres, and create an area close to the mainland from which expeditions could be launched quickly to control rebellions. Montgomery appeared to have no difficulty in attracting Scots to north Co. Down. Many of them were already wealthy landowners and very quickly the area became an extension of the Scottish Lowlands. Montgomery used the old priory as a temporary residence and began to build a typical Jacobean town. In 1613 Newtownards was created a borough, with Montgomery as its provost, and was given the right to send two representatives to the Irish Parliament in Dublin. The Montgomery family later made an enemy of Cromwell and was forced to sell its lands to Captain Robert Colville.

By the end of the seventeenth century High Street was extended into the present Mill Street, and other streets constructed at this time were Greenwell Street, Movilla Street and Market Street. The centre of the town was the market cross at the end of High Street. The Colvilles controlled the town from 1701 until 1744 when Robert's grandson sold his estates to Alexander Stewart for £4,200. As the eighteenth century progressed times became prosperous with the establishment of a linen industry. There was increased civic pride on the part of the town's landlord and its people and Stewart decided that a new town centre should be built. In 1770 the town was redesigned with the centre being at Conway Square. From it streets ran north, south, east and west, and were named accordingly.

Throughout the nineteenth century the town continued to expand. New streets were laid out to house handloom weavers and other mill workers. Many new churches were built to cater for the spiritual needs of the people. In the twentieth century factories were built and there was further expansion of the suburban areas. With the increased use of the motor car the role of Newtownards began to change from that of a market centre to a dormitory town for Belfast. The population increased from 14,000 to 24,000 during the 1970s and '80s. In 1973 local government reorganisation took place; the municipal borough ceased to exist and Ards Borough Council came into being. As a result the town was without its own government for the first time since 1613. However, Newtownards continues to expand and currently has a population of around 27,500.

The intersection of Upper North Street and Talbot Street, viewed from the railway station sometime before 1912. In those days few houses would have had the luxury of a greenhouse such as the one that can be seen in one of the gardens. In the 1930s houses were built on the wasteland to the rear of the houses on Marquis Street. The spire belongs to Strean Presbyterian Church, which was founded in 1866 and is still in existence. The other church, towards the centre of the picture, is the 2nd Newtownards Presbyterian Church, the congregation of which was originally the Bangor Congregation of the Anti-Burgher Seceders.

Frances Street, looking west towards the Market House. The street is named after Alexander Stewart's daughter-in-law, Lady Sarah Frances Seymour-Conway. It is a broad, spacious thoroughfare with many attractive buildings. Price's Lane runs off to the right, while the first shop with its awning out is the Newtownards Co-operative (this was also its registered office). The end of the terrace has been demolished and a new building housing the Ards Evangelical Bookshop built in its place. Past the Market House at the far end, the road becomes Regent Street.

A view slightly further east along Frances Street, with the church hall of the 1st Newtownards Presbyterian Church on the right. Built in 1899 at a cost of £2,000, it stands next door to the church which is set above the road and behind the wall to the hall's right. The church was built in 1834. The Rev. Dr William Wright was minister from 1879 to 1919.

A view to the east, taken from the Market House and looking along Frances Street. This was formerly known as Back Street, before the building of the Market House in 1770. The building on the right-hand side, just before the premises of W.L. Doggart, the undertaker, was formerly the meeting house of the Non-subscribing Presbyterian Church. This gave the name to the adjacent Meeting House Lane which leads to High Street. The building eventually became the Palace Cinema, then the Ritz Cinema, and eventually Wright's Arcade, containing a number of small shops. The dominating building on the left-hand side is the 1st Presbyterian Church. Gallows Hill is in the distance.

Regent Street, pictured here in 1952, was part of the town improvements after the building of the Market House. It was named after the Prince of Wales, regent from 1811 to 1820. Early in the nineteenth century it became part of the new coach road from Belfast to Donaghadee via Bradshaw's Brae. It also formed part of the Ards Tourist Trophy circuit from 1928 to 1936, when the cars and drivers were protected from the walls of the Market House by sand bags. The former Belfast Bank on the left, built in 1854, dominates the north side on the corner of Mary Street. It is now used as offices for an insurance company.

Conway Square was created in front of the new Market House in the early 1770s and, like Frances Street, was also named after Alexander Stewart's daughter-in-law, Lady Sarah Frances Seymour-Conway. In this view a fruit market is under way with apples advertised at 4½d. per quarter stone! The motorised transport on the right-hand side of the Square belongs to A. M. & H. Thompson of Newtownards Road, Belfast, and High Street, Ballynahinch. The ground floor of the Market House was originally an open square with access through six arches which are now windows. The upper floor of the west wing was an assembly room.

This early view shows the weekly market in front of the Market House, which was built to a 1765 Grecian–Doric design by Ferdinando Stratford. Initially, North Street entered Conway Square through the central archway which was fitted with gates that could be closed at night. On either side of this passageway were prison cells. By the 1890s the building was used as a town hall and it was presented to Newtownards by Lord Londonderry in 1897. Markets were part of the Plantation theory and the market day in Newtownards continues to be a Saturday.

Looking south from the Market House over the intersection of High Street and Conway Square. The Bank of Ireland building on the left remains unchanged. The fine dwelling house situated between O'Prey's paint shop and Moore Brothers' hardware store is the manse of Greenwell Street Presbyterian Church. The chimney at Walker's Mill, along with the water tank which supplied pressurised water for the mill's sprinkler system, is to the top left. The mill was built by George Walker in 1865. To its right is the military camp which, prior to the First World War, was used by the North Down Contingent of the Ulster Volunteers, the 13th Irish Rifles, and later by the police. There are currently plans to redevelop this site as an industrial and retail park.

Measuring 120 yards north to south and 90 yards east to west, Conway Square is the largest open space to be found in any Ulster town. High Street, seen here extending up to the Market Cross, forms its southern boundary and was one of the town's original streets.

Conway Square, looking south towards Scrabo Hill. The coach belongs to the McCartneys, who operated a service to and from Belfast. Such was the intensity of competition between local companies that each bus company had a different pick-up point in Belfast. The McCartneys' terminus was in Cromac Square. South Street leads off the Square towards Comber. On the corner is McEndoo, the draper. This property was previously owned by W. Laird, tailor, although by this time the upper storey had been modified with rounded corners and an arched window. Next door to it a large charabanc is parked outside Apperson's Temperance Hotel. The left-hand side of this building was later to become the RUC station.

A view looking east along High Street towards the Market Cross. Since the seventeenth century this has been the principal street in the town, with many merchants and traders as well as houses. The large building to the right is the Northern Bank, while the house at the far end, facing up the street, just past the Market Cross on the right side of the road, was once the Londonderry Estate Office from which Lord Londonderry's agent ran the estate.

Market crosses were built in many Ulster towns as a symbol of the successful establishment of a market. The original cross in Newtownards was built in 1636 and was rebuilt after destruction by Cromwell's troops in 1653. It is now the only surviving seventeenth century market cross in Ulster. An octagonal building, it is about twenty feet high and topped with a weather vane. Each of the panels on the side of the cross has a carving and these include images of a rose, a helmet with the horns of a half moon, a fleur-de-lys within a laurel wreath, a cross within a coronet, and the Shaw, Montgomery, Royal and Irish coats of arms.

A view, prior to 1914, looking up Mary Street at its intersection with Regent Street. The large building on the left is the Belfast Bank. Built in 1854, this was the town's first bank. Designed by Lanyon and Lynn, it is of Italianate design and built in Scrabo stone. A cart with a very large load of hay is at the crossroads with West Street, and to the right is Strean Church and its lecture hall. Thomas Strean invited a number of dissenters from the First Newtownards Presbyterian Church to set up a new church and he donated £5,000 in 1866. The church was designed by John Boyd of Belfast and built by John Hanna of Newtownards. Completed in 1867, its spire of 130 feet is the highest in the district.

Church Street, Newtownards.

This view was taken from the railway bridge and shows where Church Street meets Frederick Place on the western outskirts of the town. The crowds and the stalls are all part of the Reverend McIlwrath's Greenwell Street Presbyterian Church fête. As many as 2,000 children from all denominations were led out past here by Rev. McIlwrath, who always wore a top hat, on their way to Milecross where a great picnic, with races and games, was held.

17

South Street viewed from Conway Square. The street was constructed in 1770 as part of the town's redevelopment and leads south to Comber. High Street runs to the right and left. On the right-hand corner are the premises of W.G. McEndoo, a draper and milliner. The wonderful curved windows were added some time after 1903 and they provided great vantage points for the spectators of the Tourist Trophy races as the cars raced through Conway Square on their way to Comber. The T.T. races began in 1928, but were discontinued after a car crash caused fatalities among the spectators in 1936.

Around 1244 the Dominicans founded a priory on the edge of town, on what is now Court Street. The priory is 96 feet long and 24 feet wide, and was originally one storey high. After the priory was dissolved in 1541, it fell into ruin although the property was later granted to Hugh, the first Viscount Montgomery. The tower was built around 1607 as part of his residence. In 1860 the roofless priory church was consecrated as a burial ground and the interior laid out as a garden which was used by the Londonderry family and in 1970 the family transferred care of the priory to the Department of the Environment. The edge of the war memorial park is marked by the railings on the opposite side of the street.

Viewed from its intersection with East Street, Victoria Avenue runs west until it merges with Balfour Street. The town was expanding both to the north and to the west when the sod-cutting for Victoria Avenue began in April 1887. As it passed the railway station, it was originally to be called Railway Avenue, but as Queen Victoria's Golden Jubilee had just taken place its name was changed accordingly. Houses and villas were built there for professional and merchant families and it became one of the town's most fashionable addresses.

A view down North Street, towards the Market House, from the intersection with Mark Street. Ann Street, now called Orchard Lane, is to the left. The railings on the left belong to the St Patrick's Roman Catholic Church, built by Lord Londonderry in 1875. Further down on the left-hand side, with the tall front, is Templar Hall which belonged to the Order of Good Templars. When the order left, the building was taken over by the Salvation Army. The hall was built in 1875 and eventually became a hemstitching factory for G.R. Woods in 1976. It is now vacant. John Burrow's bicycle shop is situated on the right-hand corner, while the building two doors down, with the lamp and sign outside it, is the Railway Bar. The railway station was just a short walk away and as this was the last place where some travellers to Scotland or England could get a drink, the letters SSP – standing for 'short sea passage' – were above the door. The Railway Bar is still in business today.

Newtownards' first railway station was opened on 6 May 1850 and was situated opposite the Strangford Arms Hotel on Church Street. It was on the railway from Belfast to Comber. After line extensions, the station moved to a larger site at Victoria Avenue above Talbot Street in 1860, seen here prior to 1920. The line eventually closed in April 1950, when a Mr McCrory was the stationmaster, and later the station site was used for the building of a technical college, now North Down and Ards Institute.

A great view of the station which sat high on an embankment overlooking the town. The town-side platform on the left was for trains to Belfast and a comfortable waiting room with a fire was on this side. Unusually, passengers were required to cross to the other platform via a subway under the line.

A horse and cart makes its way into Newtownards from the Belfast Road. A good road was important in the plans to develop Donaghadee as the main passenger and mail port in Ulster. The Irish Post Office commissioned a new coach road from Dundonald on the outskirts of Belfast, via Bradshaw's Brae, and this was opened in 1817, serving as the main road until the modern dual carriageway was opened. While the railway bridge has long been demolished, the fine houses in view beyond it remain.

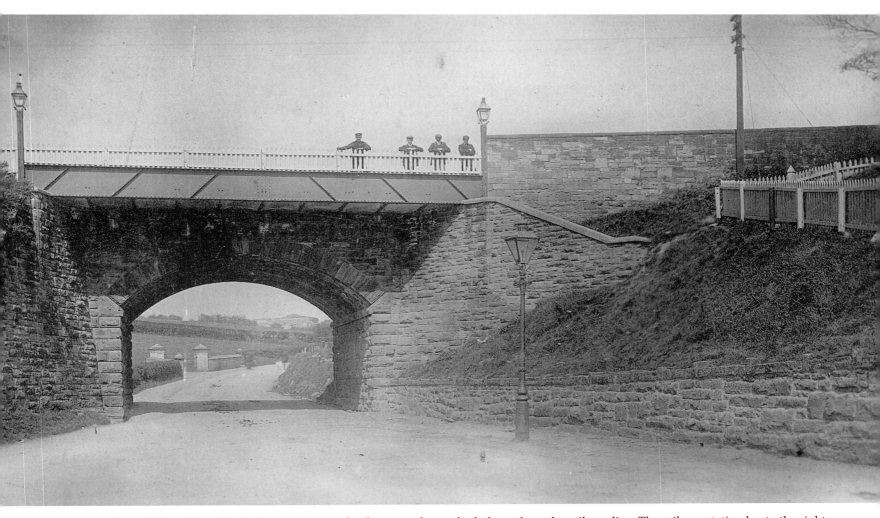

Looking towards North Road from North Street, a group of railway employees look down from the railway line. The railway station lay to the right. The bridge was demolished when the railway ceased operating and the North Down and Ards Institute is now on this site. The large gateway in the background was the entrance to the home of George Walker the mill owner.

A horse and rider tackling the Double Bank at the annual Newtownards Horticultural Association's horse-jumping competition and flower show. Horse jumping was added to the programme in 1876. The show was an important occasion and brought many visitors to the town. As can be seen here, the railway embankment provided a natural grandstand for the many spectators.

The Newtownards Horticultural Association was founded in 1854 and was the oldest recreational society in the town. It held its annual show in Dickson's Nursery, now the site of the Ards Shopping Centre. The society owed its success to Alexander Dickson, a Scotsman who set up a seed shop in High Street in 1836, and his company later became internationally renowned for its rose bushes.

The road out of town to the east was the Shore Road, now the Portaferry Road. Seen here prior to 1911, it had not been properly surfaced and the ruts of the carts are obvious. As this led out to the shores of Strangford Lough it was a popular route for the townsfolk, especially on a Sunday when it would have been busy with cyclists and walkers. This place is close to the floodgates at the head of the lough.

Pictured around 1915, the remains of the thirteenth century Augustinian Movilla Abbey are situated on the Dublin Road just outside Newtownards. The site was first attributed to St Finian who died in AD 579, although the abbey continued in use until the general dissolution of the monasteries during the reign of King Henry VIII. Within its walls are coffin lids from early Christian and Anglo–Norman graves and also buried there is Newtownards' most famous soldier, Lt. Col. Blair Mayne DSO, *Legion d'Honneur*, *Croix de Guerre*. Born in 1915, he became one of the most decorated soldiers of the Second World War. He earned four Distinguished Service Orders and was a co-founder of the Special Air Service. He died in 1955. The large headstone which can be found against the wall was erected by Sarah Donaldson of Ballyharry, in memory of her husband, John Donaldson, who died in 1851.

Movilla Cemetery is situated beside the Abbey and this view, taken from the entrance gate, is easily recognisable today. It is a large cemetery which has many early gravestones, mainly due to the fact that there are no church graveyards in the town. Persons of all denominations were buried here and there are over 200 gravestones dating from before 1800, and 750 dating from between 1800 and 1864.

The station had a large goods yard which was accessed from Victoria Avenue. It also had a turntable for the engines. In addition to being the main distribution point for the area, it was also the main point for coal importation into Newtownards with the main customer being the local gasworks (which closed in the 1970s). Nothing remains of the station or yard today. The large church with the spire is St Patrick's Roman Catholic Church, built in 1875.

Scrabo Tower on Scrabo Hill was built in memory of General Charles William Stewart-Vane, the third Marquis of Londonderry. He was a renowned diplomat and soldier. A competition for the design was set up and various architects submitted to it. The final cost was £3,010 and the tower stands 135 feet high. This view on Scrabo Road is hardly recognisable today as there are now many trees and a number of houses. Close to where the cart with the milk churns is passing was a small railway which was used to bring stone down from the Scrabo quarries.

The game of 'goff' was recorded in the Newtownards area as early as the seventeenth century. However, the modern game did not begin at the Scrabo Golf Club until 1908 when G.L. Baillie, formerly of Musselburgh and a founder member of Royal Belfast Golf Club, was paid the grand sum of two guineas to lay out a nine-hole course. The idea of a golf course here was the dream of Gerald Nettlefield and Hugh Simms. This is the clubhouse prior to 1914. The course was increased to eighteen holes in 1971.

Ards Airport, the first commercial one in Ulster, was opened on 31 August 1934 by the Governor of Northern Ireland, the Duke of Abercorn. Also in attendance at the ceremony were the seventh Lord Londonderry and Lady Marie Bury. The ground was leased from Lord Londonderry for one shilling per year, a figure that was raised to £6 in 1949. In 1935 the airport became the customs airport for Northern Ireland and all foreign traffic had to land here. The flying club's pavilion, situated close to the Comber Road, was built by Lord Londonderry and it is thought that both the Avro Cadet plane on the right and the white car belonged to him. The other two planes are De Havilland Dragon Rapides which were used for carrying passengers to the British mainland. With the development of two airports in Belfast, the aerodrome here was initially closed, but the establishment of the Ulster Flying Club in 1953, supported by Short Brothers the aircraft builders as well as the Civil Aviation Authority, secured its future. Perhaps its most famous visitor was Joachim von Ribbentrop, Hitler's Ambassador to Britain, who landed in 1937 on his way to visit the Londonderrys at Mountstewart House.

Before the days of the drive on/off cross-channel ferries, Silver City flew vehicle-carrying aircraft from Newtownards to Castle Kennedy near Stranraer. Here, a small car is being loaded through the nose doors of a Bristol freighter. Each plane carried two cars and the service began with daily flights to Scotland in April 1965 and lasted for about eighteen months. Two factors led to its demise: the fuel shortage following the Suez Crisis and the fact that the Vauxhall car company began to fly stocks of cars into Nutt's Corner Airport. This photograph appeared on a postcard posted in 1957 and shortly after this more car ferries were introduced on the Irish Sea routes. Noel O'Neill, a member of the Ulster Flying Club since 1959, learned to fly in the Auster Autocrat plane to the left.

A wonderful view of the Model School which ranked as one of the town's most impressive buildings. Built on a 2-acre site rented from Lord Londonderry in 1857, it opened in 1862. Model Schools were intended to be different from National Schools and were used to train teachers. At one time the fees were five shillings per year. There was boarding for both male and female students and they were fed from the kitchen garden. Today, it is the Newtownards Model Primary School. The building to the extreme right on Circular Road, not part of the school, has been demolished.

A great photograph of the pupils at Castle Gardens School. This was established by George Walker in 1882 for 'the benefit of the children of his employees'. While most of the children are well clothed, some are barefoot! The close proximity to the Castle Gardens Mills, opened by George Walker & Co. Ltd in 1865, is obvious. The school closed in 2002.

During the eighteenth century lead was discovered on this site at Ballyleidy by a farmer ploughing his field. A mining company was set up, but as a result of poor returns it collapsed and the mines lay abandoned from 1787 to 1827. However, the industry revived and by 1852 production of ore reached its peak with 1,420 tons being excavated. The lead content of the ore was as high as 80 per cent, but it remained difficult to mine. Since that time various attempts have been made to open up the seams, but without success. Some 200,000 tons of the waste material from the mining of the 1800s was used during the Second World War to build roads and runways at military camps and airfields. This view is of the North Mine, showing the Conlig shaft and the North Engine shaft.

Defences against flooding of the town were built by Lord Londonderry in 1811 at the head of Strangford Lough. This was part of a land reclamation scheme which allowed an additional 200 acres to be turned into arable farmland. This area is now part of a major wildlife reserve. Up to 20,000 pale-bellied geese arrive each October after travelling 3,000 kilometres from Arctic Canada.

At the head of Strangford Lough there is a floodgate and a bridge under which flows the Lower Drainage Canal. The canal was designed to drain surface water away from the town. As the town is low lying there was a health hazard before the drainage was improved. The canal runs right through the town, in some places open and in others covered. In December 1982 the barriers were breached and the town was flooded as far as the Market Cross.

The floodgates were necessary to prevent flooding of the town during high tides. They were also a popular place to visit. This photograph appears to have been taken on a Sunday as it looks like a gospel meeting was taking place. The house belonging to the operator of the floodgates is on the left, but was demolished around 1978. The National Trust controls this part of the shoreline and a car park is adjacent to this spot, enabling the many birdwatchers access to the shore.

Mount Stewart House is situated on the shores of Strangford Lough. The present house was built between 1840 and 1850, and incorporates an earlier eighteenth century structure. It was the birthplace in 1769 of Robert Stewart, who, as Lord Castlereagh, became a famous politician. Over the years the Londonderry family have played host to many prominent political figures. However, it is the gardens on the other side of the house which have made Mount Stewart famous. They were largely the creation of Edith, the wife of the seventh Marquis of Londonderry, who from 1921 designed them as a series of outdoor rooms. The estate runs to some 96 acres.

To the west of the Crawfordsburn Road a number of factories were built. To the left was the Ards Weaving Company owned by W.H. Webb. This factory was established in 1882 and had at one time 250 looms powered by a steam engine; in 1886 it employed 220 people. This site is now occupied by the Crawfordsburn Road industrial estate. To its right is the Glen Print Works. Seen from the intersection with Hartford Link, the block of houses on the right, Red Row, was built for mill workers and still stands.

In 1920 a group of young men were so impressed with the playing of the pipes by local man William John Barbour that they decided to form a band. It was formally founded in May 1922, with founding members including James Napier, Sam McAuley, Robert J. McMillan, James Anderson and, of course, W.J. Barbour. Around this time the Rev. Dr William Wright, the much revered minister of First Newtownards Presbyterian Church, died and his family gave permission to name the band the Dr William Wright Memorial Band in his honour. They are seen here on Church Street prior to their first public engagement at the 12th July celebrations at Bangor in 1923. William Barbour was pipe-major and James Anderson played the bass drum. Later they purchased full Scottish uniforms with the Gordon tartan kilt which they wear to this day. The band became world champions in 1998.

The Church Army has been at the heart of evangelism within the established church since 1882, after being founded by Wilson Carlile. The County Down II group had a horse-drawn caravan, painted with biblical texts, in which they toured the area bringing their message to the masses.

The Salvation Army were not popular when they first arrived in Newtownards. In August 1880 an editorial in the *Newtownards Chronicle* described them as 'a body of militant males and females'! They set up their headquarters in the Good Templar Hall in North Street. The editorial continued, 'it is intolerable to have them day after day, night after night, parading through our thoroughfares with hideously unmusical noises and escorted by the choicest ragamuffins in town.' The local group of the Church Army in this picture certainly don't seem to fit this description!

When King Edward VII and Queen Alexandra visited Newtownards on 25 July 1903 this was the first visit of a reigning monarch. In this photograph the Marquis and the Marchioness of Londonderry are passing through Conway Square to meet the visitors at the station. Stands were placed around the Square. One in front of the Market House charged £1 per spectator. Because of this it was mostly empty, but shortly before the arrival of their majesties it was overrun by a number of locals and was soon full, much to the chagrin of the elite of the town who had occupied the front row. The Marchioness had 274 servants to keep her guests happy at Mountstewart.

Souvenir of the Children's Celebration at Newtownards.

CORONATION DAY.

KING GEORGE V.

JUNE 22nd, 1911.

QUEEN MARY.

WITH THE COMPLIMENTS OF THE "NEWTOWNARDS CHRONICLE."

This postcard was issued with the compliments of the *Newtownards Chronicle* as a souvenir of the Children's Celebration at Newtownards of the coronation of King George V. The royal couple's close connection with the town began in September 1897 when, as the Duke and Duchess of York, they visited Mount Stewart and travelled to Newtownards in the new railway company's director's saloon.